1001 COOL JOKES

Illustrated by Glen Singleton

hinkler

hinkler

Published by Hinkler Pty Ltd
45–55 Fairchild Street
Heatherton Victoria 3202 Australia
www.hinkler.com

© Hinkler Pty Ltd 2004, 2013, 2023

Illustrated by Glen Singleton
Cover design by Hinkler Books Design Studio
Typeset by MPS Limited

ISBN: 978 1 4889 2492 7

Printed and bound in China

CONTENTS

ANIMALS

1 What do you get when you cross an elephant with a fish?

Swimming trunks!

2 What happened when the dog went to the flea circus?

He stole the show!

3 What did the dog say when he was attacked by a tiger?

Nothing, dogs can't talk.

4 How did the skunk call his mother?

On a smell phone.

5 **What do you get if you cross a cocker spaniel with a rooster and a poodle?**

Cockerpoodledoo.

6 **Why are four-legged animals bad dancers?**

Because they have two left feet.

7 **What do you call a woodpecker with no beak?**

A headbanger.

8 **What do you get when you cross a mountain lion and a parrot?**

I don't know, but when it talks, you had better listen!

9 **What do you get when you cross a chicken and a caterpillar?**

Drumsticks for everyone!

10 **What do you call a lamb with a machine gun?**

Lambo.

11   **What do you get when you cross a high chair and a bird?**

A stool pigeon.

12   **What do cats put in soft drinks?**

Mice cubes.

13   **What's 150 feet long and jumps every ten seconds?**

A dinosaur with the hiccups.

14   **What do you call a camel with three humps?**

Humphrey.

15   **What do you call a penguin in the desert?**

Lost.

16   **What do you get if you sit under a cow?**

A pat on the head.

17 **What do you call a duck with fangs?**

Count Quackula.

18 **What did Mr. and Mrs. Chicken call their baby?**

Egg.

Isn't he gorgeous... Let's call him... EGG

19 **What kind of tie do pigs wear?**

A pigsty.

20 **Why don't turkeys get invited to dinner parties?**

Because they use fowl language.

21 **Which side of the chicken has the most feathers?**

The outside.

GOBBLE *@?!!×※ GOBBLE... GOBBLE GOBBLE GOBBLE

22 **What did the duck say when she finished shopping?**

Just put it on my bill.

23   **What do frozen cows do?**

They give ice cream.

24   **What is a dog's favorite food?**

Anything that is on your plate!

25   **What did the hen say when she saw scrambled eggs?**

What a crazy mixed-up kid.

26   **Why didn't the rooster cross the road?**

Because he was chicken!

27   **Why did the cow jump over the moon?**

Because the farmer had cold hands.

28   **Why do mother kangaroos hate rainy days?**

Because their kids have to play inside.

29 **Why did the chicken cross the basketball court?**

He heard the referee calling fowls.

30 **What do you call an elephant in a telephone box?**

Stuck.

31 **What do you call an elephant that never washes?**

A smellyphant.

32 **What do you give a sick elephant?**

A very big paper bag.

33 **What's black and very noisy?**

A crow with a drum set.

34 **Why do elephants live in the jungle?**

Because they can't fit inside houses.

35 **Why are elephants wrinkled all over?**

Because they can't fit on an ironing board.

36   **Why are skunks always arguing?**
Because they like to make a big stink!

37   **What do you call a cow riding a skateboard?**
A cow-tastrophe about to happen.

38   **What do you get if you cross a parrot with a shark?**
An animal that talks your head off!

39   **Why did the elephant paint the bottom of his feet yellow?**
So he could hide upside down in custard.

40   **Have you ever found an elephant in custard?**
No.
It must work then!

41   **What's black and white and eats like a horse?**
A zebra.

42   **What do get if you cross a centipede with a parrot?**
A walkie-talkie.

43   **What did the snail say when he hitched a ride on the turtle's back?**
Weeeeeeeeeeeeeeeeeeeeee!!!!

44   **What do you get if you cross a duck with a rooster?**
A bird that wakes you up at the quack of dawn!

45 Did you hear the one about the dog running ten miles to retrieve a stick?

It was too far-fetched.

46 What's black and white and black and white and black and white?

A penguin rolling down a hill!

47 What do dogs and trees have in common?

Bark!

48 What is white, fluffy, and lives in the jungle?

A meringue-utan!

49 What's bright orange and sounds like a parrot?

A carrot!

50   **What's tall, hairy, lives in the Himalayas, and does 500 sit-ups a day?**

The abdominal snowman!

51   **What is a slug?**

A snail with a housing problem.

52   **What do you get if you cross a skunk with a bear?**

Winnie the Poo.

53   **What's the difference between an elephant and a flea?**

An elephant can have fleas, but a flea can't have elephants.

54   **Did you know it takes three sheep to make a sweater?**
Hmmm. I didn't even know they could knit.

55   **What would you do if a bull charged you?**
Pay him cash.

56   **What steps would you take if a bull chased you?**
Big ones.

57   **What happened to the dog that swallowed the watch?**
He got ticks.

58   **Why is the sky so high?**
So birds won't bump their heads.

59   **Why do giraffes have long necks?**

Because their feet stink.

60   **What's striped and goes around and around?**

A zebra on a merry-go-round.

61   **Where do bees go when they're sick?**

To the waspital!

62   **How do you milk a mouse?**

You can't, the bucket won't fit underneath!

63   **What time is it when you see a crocodile?**

Time to run.

64 **What time is it when an elephant sits on your fence?**

Time to get a new fence.

65 **What shouldn't you do when you meet a shark?**

Go to pieces.

66 **What do you call a baby whale?**

A little squirt.

67 **What are feathers good for?**

Birds.

68 **What do you get if you run over a sparrow with a lawn mower?**

Shredded tweet.

69 **What animal drops from the clouds?**

A raindeer.

70 **Are you a vegetarian because you love animals?**

No, it's because I don't like plants.

71 **Why did they cross a homing pigeon with a parrot?**

So if it got lost it could ask for directions.

72 **What has four legs and goes "Boo"?**

A cow with a cold.

73 **What do you call fourteen rabbits hopping backward?**

A receding hareline.

74 **Why do gorillas have big nostrils?**

Because they have big fingers.

75 **What do you call a fly with no wings?**

A walk.

76 **What do you get if you cross a chicken with a yo-yo?**

A bird that lays the same egg three times!

77 **When is it bad luck to see a black cat?**

When you're a mouse.

78 **What's black and white and goes around and around?**

A penguin caught in a revolving door.

79 **Why are elephants gray?**

So you can tell them apart from canaries.

80 **What do leopards say after lunch?**

"That sure hit the spots!"

81 **What did the canary say when she laid a square egg?**

Ouch!

Better move to the other side of the street

82 **Why did the dog cross the street?**

To slobber on the other side.

83 **What's the difference between a barking dog and an umbrella?**

You can shut the umbrella up.

84 **Why are dogs like hamburgers?**

They're both sold by the pound.

85 **What did the duck say to the comedian after the show?**

You really quacked me up!

86 **Why do birds fly south?**

It's too far to walk!

87 **What do you give a pig with a rash?**

Oinkment!

88   Ten cats were on a boat, one jumped off, how many were left?

None, they were all copycats!

89   Why did the chicken cross the road?

To see the man laying bricks.

90   What's black and white and makes a terrible noise?

A penguin playing the bagpipes.

91   What's a pelican's favorite dish?

Anything that fits the bill.

92 **What do you get when you cross an elephant with a sparrow?**

Broken telephone poles everywhere.

93 **What do you call a huge pile of cats?**

A meowntain.

94 **Who went into the tiger's lair and came out alive?**

The tiger.

95 **How do you start a flea race?**

One, two, flea, go!

96 **What do frogs order in restaurants?**

French flies!

97 Why does a hummingbird hum?

It doesn't know the words!

98 Did you put the cat out?

I didn't know it was on fire!

99 How do you know that carrots are good for your eyesight?

Have you ever seen a rabbit wearing glasses?

The rabbit who wouldn't eat his carrots as a child...

100 What does a crab use to call someone?

A shell phone!

101 **What has four legs and sees just as well from both ends?**

A horse with his eyes closed.

102 **What do you call a sleeping bull?**

A bulldozer!

103 **What do you get when you cross a cat with a lemon?**

A sour puss!

104 **What kind of cat shouldn't you play cards with?**

A cheetah!

105 **Hickory dickory dock,**

Three mice ran up the clock,

The clock struck one,

But the other two got away with minor injuries.

106 **What do you give a dog with a fever?**

Mustard: it's the best thing for a hot dog!

107 **Why do cows wear bells?**

Because their horns don't work!

108 **What is gray, has big ears, and a trunk?**

A mouse going on vacation!

109 **What did the porcupine say to the cactus?**

Are you my mother?

110 **What happened to the snake with a cold?**

She adder viper nose.

111 **How can you stop moles digging up your garden?**

Hide the shovel.

112 **What's the difference between a unicorn and a lettuce?**

One is a funny beast and the other a bunny feast.

113 **What would you get if you crossed a chicken with a mild-mannered reporter?**

Cluck Kent.

114 **What do you get when you cross a rabbit with a shellfish?**

The oyster bunny.

115 **What is brown, has a hump, and lives in the North Pole?**

A very lost camel!

116 **What do you call a group of boring, spotted dogs?**

101 Dull-matians!

117 **Why can't a leopard hide?**

Because he's always spotted!

118 **What did scientists say when they found bones on the moon?**

The cow didn't make it!

119 **What cat has eight legs?**

An octopuss.

120 **What kind of dog tells the time?**

A watch dog!

121 **How do you stop a rhino from charging?**
Take away its credit card!

122 **What do you call a pony with a sore throat?**
A little horse!

123 **What's the difference between a piano and a fish?**
You can tune a piano, but you can't tuna fish!

124 **What do you do with a blue whale?**
Try to cheer him up!

125 **Where do sheep go to get haircuts?**
To the baa-baa shop!

126 **What looks like half a cat?**
The other half!

127 **Why can't an elephant ride a tricycle?**

Because they don't have thumbs to ring the bell!

128 **How do you fit an elephant into a matchbox?**

Take out the matches!

129 **How do you fit a tiger into a matchbox?**

Take out the elephant!

130 **What is gray with sixteen wheels?**

An elephant on roller skates!

131   **Did you know that elephants never forget?**

What do they have to remember!

132   **Why is a snail stronger than an elephant?**

A snail carries its house, and an elephant only carries his trunk!

133   **Why is an elephant large, gray, and wrinkled?**

Because if it was small, white, and smooth, it would be an aspirin!

134   **What did one firefly say to the other before he left?**

Bye! I'm glowing now!

135   **Why was the father centipede so upset?**

All of the kids needed new shoes!

2 million pairs of shoes!!

136 **What do you call a mad flea?**
A looney-tic!

137 **What kinds of bees fight?**
Rumblebees!

138 **What type of dog does a magician have?**
A labracadabrador.

139 **Why was the bee's hair sticky?**
Because he used a honey-comb!

140 **Why did the snail paint an S on its car?**
So people would say, "Look at that S car go!"

141 **What do you call two spiders who just got married?**

Newlywebs!

142 **If a snake and an undertaker got married, what would they put on their towels?**

Hiss and Hearse!

143 **What are six things smaller than an ant's mouth?**

Six of its teeth!

144 **How do bees travel?**

They take the buzz!

145 **How do you make a snake cry?**

Take away its rattle!

146 **Why did the firefly get bad grades in school?**

He wasn't very bright!

147 **What's worse than finding a worm in your apple?**

Finding half a worm!

148 **Where do you put a noisy dog?**

In a barking lot!

149 **What did the caterpillar say to the butterfly?**

You'll never get me up in one of those things.

150 **What do you call a fly when it retires?**

A flew.

151 **How can you tell an elephant from a banana?**

Try to lift it up. If you can't, it's either an elephant or a very heavy banana.

152 **What do you get when you cross an elephant with peanut butter?**

Either an elephant that sticks to the roof of your mouth or peanut butter that never forgets.

153 **What game do elephants play in a Mini?**

Squash!

154 **What do you call a monkey with a banana in each ear?**

Anything, he can't hear you.

155   Why do tigers eat raw meat?

Because they can't cook.

156   Now you see it, now you don't, now you see it, now you don't. What is it?

A black cat on a zebra crossing.

157   What is big, green, and has a trunk?

An unripe elephant.

158 **What happened when the cow jumped over the barbed wire fence?**

It was an udder catastrophe!

159 **What do you call a young female moth?**

Myth.

160 **How does an elephant get down from a tree?**

He sits on a leaf and waits for fall.

161 **What do you get from nervous cows?**

Milkshakes.

162 **What do you get if you cross an alligator with a camera?**

A snapshot.

163 **Why do elephants' tusks stick out?**

Because their parents can't afford braces!

164 **What's the biggest moth in the world?**

A mam-moth.

165 **What's the biggest mouse in the world?**

A hippopotamouse.

166 **What do you get when you cross a rabbit with a snake?**

A jump rope.

167 **Why didn't the piglets listen to their father?**
Because he was a boar.

168 **Where can you buy ancient elephants?**
At a mammoth sale.

169 **Why did the lion spit out the clown?**
Because he tasted funny.

170 **What did the beaver say to the tree?**
It's been nice gnawing you.

171   How do you make toast in the jungle?
Put your bread under a gorilla.

172   What was the tortoise doing on the freeway?
About three miles an hour.

That's my funny bone!

173   How do tell which end of a worm is the head?
Tickle him in the middle and watch where he smiles.

174   What do you give a sick bird?
Tweetment.

175   How do you stop an elephant from smelling?
Tie a knot in his trunk.

176 **What has two legs and two tails?**

A lizard flipping a coin.

177 **How do you hire a horse?**

Put four bricks under his feet.

178 **What should you know if you want to be a lion tamer?**

More than the lion.

179 **Why did the fly fly?**

Because the spider spied her.

180 **What's bright blue and very heavy?**

An elephant holding its breath.

181   What did the skunk say when the wind changed direction?

Ahhh, it's all coming back to me now.

182   Why did the viper vipe her nose?

Because the adder 'ad 'er 'ankerchief.

183   What's the best way to catch a rabbit?

Hide in the bushes and make a noise like lettuce.

184   What goes 99 bonk?

A centipede with a wooden leg.

BONK

185   Why do cows use the doorbell?

Because their horns don't work!

SQUEAK...SQUEAK...

DING DONG

HORNS NOT WORKING!

186 **What's white on the outside, green on the inside, and hops?**

A frog sandwich.

187 **What does a porcupine have for lunch?**

A hamburger with prickles.

188 **What do get when you cross a dog and a cat?**

An animal that chases itself.

GORILLA

RABBIT

189 **How can you tell a rabbit from a gorilla?**

A rabbit looks nothing like a gorilla.

190 **What did the goose say when he got cold?**

"I have people-bumps!"

191 **What lies down a hundred feet in the air?**

A centipede.

192 **What's the difference between a well-dressed man and a tired dog?**

The man wears a suit, the dog just pants.

193 **Which famous outlaw lives at the bottom of the sea?**

Billy the Squid.

194 **What did the mosquito say when he saw a camel's hump?**

Gee, did I do that?

195 **How many skunks does it take to stink out a room?**

A phew.

196 **How do goldfish go into business?**

They start on a small scale.

197 **Why do snakes have forked tongues?**

Because they can't use chopsticks.

198 **How do you spell "mouse trap" with three letters?**

C A T.

199 **What did the dog say when he sat on the sandpaper?**

Rough, rough!

200 **What is more fantastic than a talking dog?**

A spelling bee!

201 **What do you get if you cross a giraffe with a porcupine?**

A 30-foot toothbrush.

202 **What can go as fast as a race horse?**

The jockey!

203 **If horses wear shoes, what do camels wear?**

Desert boots.

204 **What do you call a lazy baby kangaroo?**

A pouch potato.

205 **What's the same size and shape as an elephant but weighs nothing?**

An elephant's shadow.

206 **What's black and white and hides in caves?**

A zebra who owes money.

207 **Where do you find a no-legged dog?**

Right where you left it.

208 **How do you get an elephant up an acorn tree?**

Sit him on an acorn and wait twenty years.

209 **What did one flea say to the other?**

Shall we walk or take the dog?

210 **What did the cat have for breakfast?**

Mice Krispies.

211 **What goes tick ... tick ... woof?**

A watchdog.

212   Why was the chicken sick?

Because it had people pox.

213   How do you get down from an elephant?

You don't get down from an elephant, you get down from a duck.

214   What do elephants have that no other animal does?

Baby elephants.

215   What's big, white, furry, and found in outback Australia?

A very lost polar bear.

216   Why do horses only wear shoes?

Because they would look silly with socks on.

217   **How do you stop a pig from smelling?**

Put a cork in his nose.

218   **What's the difference between an African elephant and an Indian elephant?**

About 3700 miles.

DINOSAURS

219 **What do you get if you cross a dinosaur with a vampire?**

A blood shortage.

220 **What do dinosaurs put on their french fries?**

Tomatosaurus.

221 **What's extinct and works in rodeos?**

Bronco-saurus.

222   **Why did the dinosaur cross the road?**

What road?

223   **What do you call a dinosaur with high heels?**

My-feet-are-saurus.

224   **What do you get if you give a dinosaur a pogo stick?**

Big holes in your driveway.

225   **What do you call a distracted dinosaur?**

Do-ya-think-he-saw-us?

226 **What do you call a dinosaur that's a noisy sleeper?**

Brontosnorus.

227 **Why did the baby dinosaur get arrested?**

He took the bus home!

228 **What do you get when you cross a dinosaur and a pig?**

Jurassic Pork.

229 **What does a Triceratops sit on?**

Its Tricera-bottom!

230 **What do dinosaurs put on their floors?**

Rep-tiles.

231 **What dinosaur can't stay out in the rain?**

Stegosaur-rust!

232 **What do you call a group of people who dig for bones?**

A skeleton crew.

233 **What do you get when a dinosaur skydives?**

A large hole.

234 **What has a spiked tail, plates on its back, and wheels?**

A stegosaurus on roller skates.

235 **What's the difference between a dinosaur and a sandwich?**

A sandwich doesn't weigh five tons.

236 **What's worse than a Tyrannosaurus with a toothache?**

A Diplodocus with a sore throat!

237 **Why couldn't the long-necked dinosaur see?**

Because it had its head in the clouds!

Now that's an old fossil...

238 **What do you call a one-hundred-million-year-old dinosaur?**

A fossil.

239 **What do you get if you cross a dinosaur with a dog?**

A very nervous postal worker.

240 **What is found in the middle of dinosaurs?**

The letter "s."

241   **What did the egg say to the dinosaur?**
You're egg-stinct.

242   **Why didn't the dinosaur cross the road?**
Because roads weren't invented.

243   **What do you call a scared tyrannosaurus?**
A nervous rex.

244   **What dinosaur wears a cowboy hat?**
Tyrannosaurus Tex.

245   **Why don't more dinosaurs join the police force?**
They can't hide behind billboards.

246   What do you call
a dinosaur eating
a taco?

Tyrannosaurus Mex.

247   What do you call a dinosaur with magic powers?

Tyrannosaurus Hex.

248   What do you call a dinosaur that destroys everything
in its path?

Tyrannosaurus Wrecks.

MISCELLANEOUS

249 **Why is six scared of seven?**

Because 7-8-9.

250 **What did the egg say to the whisk?**

I know when I'm beaten.

251 **What is scared of wolves and swears?**

Little Rude Riding Hood.

252 **Why did the toilet paper roll down the hill?**

To get to the bottom.

253 **What's brown and sounds like a bell?**
Dung.

254 **Where are the Andes?**
At the end of your armies.

255 **What helps keep your teeth together?**
Toothpaste.

256 **What kind of tree can you fit in one hand?**
A palm tree.

257 **What do you call a ship that lies on the bottom of the ocean and shakes?**
A nervous wreck!

258 **How do you make a hotdog stand?**
Steal its chair!

259 **Why was Thomas Edison able to invent the light bulb?**

Because he was very bright.

260 **What's the best way to win a race?**

Run faster than everyone else.

261 **Can a match box?**

No, but a tin can.

262 **Where do pirates buy their hooks?**

The second hand shop.

263 **During which battle was Lord Nelson killed?**

His last one.

264 **Why did the scarecrow win a Nobel prize?**

Because she was outstanding in her field.

265 **Why did the surfer stop surfing?**

Because the sea weed.

266 **What was more useful than the invention of the first telephone?**

The second telephone.

267 **What's small and annoying?**

I don't know, but it answers to my sister's name.

268 **How do you use an Egyptian doorbell?**

Toot-and-come-in.

269 **What side of an apple is the left side?**

The side that hasn't been eaten.

270 **How can you tell a dogwood tree?**

By its bark.

271 **What invention allows you to see through walls?**

A window.

272 **What are the four letters the dentist says when a patient visits him?**

ICDK (I see decay).

273 **How did the dentist become a brain surgeon?**

His drill slipped.

274 **What's another word for tears?**

Glumdrops.

275 **Which months have 28 days?**

All of them.

276 Where does Tarzan buy his clothes?

At a jungle sale.

277 How do you make a fire with two sticks?

Make sure one of them is a match.

278 When do you put a frog in your sister's bed?

When you can't find a mouse.

279 Why did Polly put the kettle on?

She didn't have anything else to wear.

280 **What did the little light bulb say to its Mom?**

I wuv you watts and watts.

281 **Why did the teacher wear dark glasses?**

Because she had such a bright class.

282 **Why do toadstools grow so close together?**

They don't need mushroom.

283 **What did the judge say to the dentist?**

Do you swear to pull the tooth, the whole tooth, and nothing but the tooth?

284 **What happens when the Queen burps?**

She issues a royal pardon.

285 **What did one wall say to the other wall?**

I'll meet you at the corner.

286 **Where did the king keep his armies?**

Up his sleevies.

287 **Why was the math book sad?**

Because it had too many problems.

288 **What's the letter that ends everything?**

The letter G.

289 **What did the stamp say to the envelope?**

Stick with me and we will go places.

290 **What do you call a man with an elephant on his head?**

Squashed.

You can say that again.

291 **I have ten legs, twenty arms, and fifty-four feet. What am I?**

A liar.

292 **What did the tie say to the hat?**

You go on ahead, I'll just hang around.

293 What do you call a boomerang that doesn't come back to you?

A stick.

294 Where was the Declaration of Independence signed?

At the bottom.

295 Why does lightning shock people?

It doesn't know how to conduct itself.

296 What did the pencil sharpener say to the pencil?

Stop going in circles and get to the point!

297 What's the nearest thing to silver?

The Lone Ranger's bottom.

298 What do Alexander the Great and Kermit the Frog have in common?

The same middle name!

299 There are three kinds of people in the world. Those who can count. And those who can't.

300 What's the easiest way to get on TV?

Sit on it.

301 What has four legs and doesn't walk?

A table.

302 **Where do you find giant snails?**
At the ends of their fingers.

303 **Name three inventions that have helped humans go up in the world.**
The elevator, the ladder, and the alarm clock.

304 **What's brown, hairy, and has no legs but walks?**
Dad's socks.

305 **How do you saw the sea in half?**
With a sea-saw.

306 **What's easy to get into but hard to get out of?**
Trouble.

307 **Mom, why isn't my nose twelve inches long?**
Because then it would be a foot.

308 **Dad, can you see a change in me?**
No, why, son?
Because I swallowed some coins.

309 **How did the rocket lose his job?**

He was fired.

310 **What's yellow and wears a mask?**

The Lone Banana.

311 **What has many rings but no fingers?**

A telephone.

312 **What do you get if you jump into the Red Sea?**

Wet.

313 **What's brown and sticky?**

A stick.

314 **What do you call a lazy toy?**

An inaction figure.

315 Why did the balloon burst?

Because it saw the soda pop!

316 What do all the Smiths in the telephone book have in common?

They all have telephones.

317 Why do gas stations always lock their bathrooms?

They are afraid someone might clean them.

318 What do you get if you cross the Atlantic with the Titanic?

About half way.

Hey...I paid for the full trip!

TITANIC

319 Why did the bacteria cross the microscope?

To get to the other slide.

320 **What do you do if your nose goes on strike?**

Picket.

321 **What's the hardest part about sky diving?**

The ground!

322 **What's the difference between a TV and a newspaper?**

Ever tried swatting a fly with a TV?

323 **What did the little mountain say to the big mountain?**

Hi Cliff!

324 **Why did the traffic light turn red?**

You would too if you had to change in the middle of the street!

325 **How much does it cost for a pirate to get earrings?**

A buccaneer!

326 **What is the difference between a jeweler and a jailer?**

A jeweler sells watches and a jailer watches cells!

327 **What did the digital clock say to its mother?**

Look, Ma, no hands.

328 **Why didn't the man die when he drank poison?**

Because he was in the living room.

329 **What do hippies do?**

They hold your leggies on.

330 **What did Snow White say while she waited outside the photo booth?**

Some day my prints will come!

331 **What did one raindrop say to the other?**

Two's company, three's a cloud.

332 **What do you call a snowman with a suntan?**
A puddle!

333 **What did the penny say to the other penny?**
We make perfect cents.

334 **What did the Pacific Ocean say to the Atlantic Ocean?**
Nothing. It just waved.

335 **Who was the smallest man in the world?**
The guard that fell asleep on his watch.

336 **What can jump higher than a house?**
Anything, houses can't jump!

337 **Why did the bungy jumper take a vacation?**
Because he was at the end of his rope.

338 **Why did E.T. have such big eyes?**

Because he saw his phone bill.

339 **What sort of star is dangerous?**

A shooting star.

340 **Why did the belt go to jail?**

Because it held up a pair of pants.

341 **What is the name of the detective who sings quietly to himself while solving crimes?**

Sherlock Hums!

342 **Why was the butcher worried?**

His job was at steak!

343 **What's the difference between an elephant and a matterbaby?**

What's a matterbaby?

Nothing, but thanks for asking!

344 **What did the shirt say to the jeans?**
Meet you on the clothesline—that's where I hang out!

345 **What did the big hand of the clock say to the little hand?**
Got a minute?

346 **What kind of music does your father like to sing?**
Pop music.

347 **What's the easiest way to find a pin in your carpet?**
Walk around in your bare feet.

348 **What did the parents say to their son who wanted to play drums?**
Beat it!

349 **Where do you find baby soldiers?**
In the infantry.

350 Can February March?

No. But April May.

351 What's the definition of intense?

That's where campers sleep.

352 What do you call a man who stands around and makes faces all day?

A clockmaker.

353 What did one toilet say to the other toilet?

You look a bit flushed!

354 **Did you hear the one about the man who went into the cloning shop?**

When he came out, he was beside himself!

355 **What did the key say to the glue?**

"You wanna be in show biz, kid? Stick to me, I can open doors for you!"

356 **When does B come after U?**

When you take some of its honey!

357 **Why was the archaeologist upset?**

His job was in ruins!

358 **Where does a sick ship go?**

To the dock.

359 **Did I tell you the joke about the high wall?**

I'd better not, you might not get over it.

360 **What did the first mind reader say to the second mind reader?**

You're all right, how am I?

361 **What did one ear say to the other ear?**

Between you and me, we need a haircut.

362 **What flowers grow under your nose?**

Tulips.

363 **What did the ear 'ear?**

Only the nose knows.

364 **Did you know that Davy Crockett had three ears?**

A right ear, a left ear, and a wild frontier.

365 **Why does the ocean roar?**

You would too if you had crabs pinching your bottom.

366 **What will go up a drainpipe down but won't go down a drainpipe up?**

An umbrella.

367 **What would you call Superman if he lost all his powers?**

Man.

368 **What has a hundred legs but can't walk?**

Fifty pairs of pants.

369 **I have five noses, seven ears, and four mouths. What am I?**

Very ugly.

370 **What did one eye say to the other eye?**

Something that smells has come between us.

MONSTERS

371 **Little Monster: I hate my teacher's guts!**

Mommy Monster: Then just eat around them!

You wouldn't like me if I start to cry...

372 **What's green, sits in the corner, and cries?**

The Incredible Sulk.

373 **What's a vampire's favorite dog?**

A bloodhound!

374 **What do vampires cross the sea in?**

Blood vessels.

375 **What did the alien say to the gas pump?**

Take your finger out of your ear when I'm talking to you.

376 **What did King Kong say when his sister had a baby?**

Well, I'll be a monkey's uncle.

377 **Why did the zombie decide to stay in his coffin?**

He felt rotten.

378 **What happened when the abominable snowman ate a curry?**

He melted.

379 **What do you call a good-looking, kind, and considerate monster?**

A complete failure.

380 **Little Monster: Should I eat my fries with my fingers?**

Mommy Monster: No, you should eat them separately!

381 **Mom, everyone at school calls me a werewolf.**

Ignore them and comb your face.

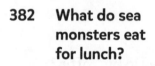

Remember... always part your face on the left, dear...

382 **What do sea monsters eat for lunch?**

Potato ships!

383 **Why did the cyclops give up teaching?**

Because he only had one pupil.

I thought it had a couple more miles left in it yet...

384 **Why do witches fly on broomsticks?**

Because it's better than walking.

385 Why did Dracula take some medicine?

To stop his coffin.

386 What do devils drink?

Demonade.

387 What don't zombies wear on boat trips?

Life jackets.

388 What do you call a sleeping monster who won't keep quiet?

Frankensnore.

389 **What happened to Frankenstein's monster when he was caught speeding?**

He was fined $50 and dismantled for six months.

390 **How does a monster count to thirteen?**

On his fingers.

391 **What happened to the monster that took the five o'clock train home?**

He had to give it back.

392 **What kind of cheese do monsters eat?**

Monsterella!

393 **What do you get when you cross a vampire and a snowman?**

Frostbite!

394 **What did the witch say to the vampire?**

Get a life.

395 **What do you call a monster that was locked in the freezer overnight?**

A cool ghoul!

396 **What do you call a single vampire?**

A bat-chelor.

397 **Mother vampire to son:**

Hurry up and eat your breakfast before it clots.

398 **What do you get when you cross a skunk with Frankenstein?**

Stinkenstein!

399 **What do you call a ten-foot-tall monster?**

Shorty!

400 **What is a vampire's favorite kind of coffee?**

De-coffin-ated!

401 How can you tell a Martian would be a good gardener?

They all have green thumbs!

402 What does a monster say when introduced?

Pleased to eat you.

403 What did the baby zombie want for his birthday?

A deady bear.

oh hello

404 Why did the sea monster eat five ships carrying potatoes?

Because you can't just eat one potato ship.

405 Why doesn't anyone kiss vampires?

Because they have bat breath.

406 **What do you think the tiniest vampire gets up to at night?**

Your ankles.

Little bloodsucker

407 **Why do ghosts go to parties?**

To have a wail of a time.

408 **Why aren't vampires welcome in blood banks?**

Because they only make withdrawals.

409 **Why do ghosts hate rain?**

It dampens their spirits.

410 **Which monsters always get indigestion?**

Goblins.

411 **Which monsters are bad at math?**

All of them ... unless you Count Dracula.

412 **What does a ghost have to get before he can scare anyone?**

A haunting license.

413 **What did one ghost say to the other?**

Don't spook until you're spooken to!

414 **What do you call a witch that lives at the beach?**

A sand witch!

415 **How do you make a witch scratch?**

Take away the W!

416 **Why do mummies have trouble keeping friends?**

They're too wrapped up in themselves.

417 **What do you get when a ghost sits in a tree?**

Petrified wood!

418 **How many witches does it take to change a light bulb?**

Just one, but she changes it into a toad!

419 **Who is the best dancer at a monster party?**

The Boogie Man!

420 **What is a monster's favorite drink?**

Ghoul-Aid!

421 **Where does a ghost go on Saturday nights?**

Somewhere he can boogie!

422 **What is a spook's favorite ride?**

A roller-ghoster!

423 **What is the difference between a huge, smelly monster and candy?**

People like candy!

424 **What is Dracula's favorite fruit?**

Necktarines!

VEGETARIAN VAMPIRES

425 **What is Dracula's favorite place in New York?**

The Vampire State Building!

426 **What is a ghost's favorite dessert?**

Boo-berries and I scream!

427 Why can't the Invisible Man pass school?

The teacher always marks him absent!

428 Why did the monster eat the North Pole?

He was in the mood for a frozen dinner!

429 When do monsters eat people?

Chewsday.

430 What is a ghost's favorite bedtime story?

Little Boo Peep!

431 What kind of mistake does a ghost make?

A boo-boo!

432 Why do they have a fence around the graveyard?

Everyone is dying to get in!

433 **What is big, hairy, and bounces up and down?**

A monster on a pogo stick!

434 **What is a ghost's favorite type of fruit?**

Boo-berry!

435 **What did the vampire say when he had bitten someone?**

It's been nice gnawing you!

436 **What did the skeleton say to the twin witches?**

Which witch is which?

437 **Why is the vampire so unpopular?**

Because he is a pain in the neck!

HI GIRLS...!

This guy is a real pain in the neck

438 **What does a ghost do when he gets in a car?**

Puts his sheet belt on!

439 **Why didn't the ghost eat liver?**

He didn't have the stomach for it!

440 **What did the baby monster say to his babysitter?**

I want my mummy!

441 **What do you call five witches on a broom?**

A car pool!

442 **Why did Dr. Jekyll cross the road?**

To get to the other Hyde!

443   **What kind of fur do you get from a werewolf?**
As fur away as you can get!

444   **Who did the monster take to the Halloween dance?**
His ghoul friend!

445   **Why did Godzilla get a ticket?**
He ran through a stomp sign!

446   **What do you call a monster sleeping in a chandelier?**
A light sleeper.

447   **What is a mummy's favorite kind of music?**
Rap!

448   **What kind of boots do spooks wear?**
Ghoulashes!

449   **Where do ghosts live?**
On dead ends!

450 **Why are ghosts such terrible liars?**

Because you can see right through them.

451 **What's a skeleton?**

Someone with their outside off and their insides out.

452 **What do you call a silly skeleton?**

A numbskull.

453 **What kind of witch turns out the lights?**

A lights-witch!

454 **What did one skeleton say to the other?**

If we had any guts, we'd get out of here!

455 **What do you call a vampire's dog?**

A bloodhound

456 **How do you know when a ghost is sad?**

He says booooooooo hooooooooo!

I hate those sad movies where the ghost gets exorcised.

457 **What do you do with a green monster?**

Put him in a paper bag till he ripens.

458 **Did you hear about the ghost who ate all the Christmas decorations?**

He got tinselitis.

459 **What do little ghosts play with?**

Deady bears.

460 **What is Dracula's favorite ice cream flavor?**

Vein-illa!

461 Why did the little monsters stay up all night?

They were studying for a blood test.

462 What do baby ghosts wear on their feet?

Boo-ties!

463 Why did the troll tell jokes to the mirror?

He wanted to see it crack up!

464 Why do skeletons play the piano in church?

Because they don't have any organs!

465 How can you tell if a vampire has a cold?

He starts coffin!

466 **What is a witch's favorite class in school?**

Spelling!

467 **What bear goes around scaring other animals?**

Winnie the Boo!

468 **What does a ghost read every day?**

His horrorscope.

469 **Where does Frankenstein's wife have her hair done?**

At the scare-dresser.

470 **What game do young ghosts love?**

Hide and shriek.

471 How does an alien congratulate someone?

He gives him a high six.

472 How do monsters like their eggs?

Terrifried.

473 Why couldn't the skeleton go to the dance?

He had no body to go with.

474 Why didn't the skeleton cross the road?

Because he didn't have the guts to!

475 Why did it take the monster ten months to finish a book?

Because he wasn't very hungry.

476 How many vampires does it take to change a light bulb?

None. They love the dark.

477 **Why are skeletons afraid of dogs?**
Because dogs like bones.

478 **What does a monster eat after he's been to the dentist?**
The dentist.

479 **Where do ghosts play golf?**
At the golf corpse.

HA
HA
HA

480 **What do you call the winner of a monster beauty contest?**
Ugly.

481 **How do you make a skeleton laugh?**
Tickle his funnybone.

482 **What do witches put in their hair?**
Scare spray.

483   Why are skeletons usually so calm?

Nothing gets under their skin!

484   What do ghosts eat for dinner?

Spook-etti.

485   Why don't skeletons wear shorts?

Because they have bony knees.

486   Do zombies have trouble getting dates?

No, they can usually dig someone up.

487   What does a boy monster do when a girl monster rolls her eyes at him?

He rolls them back to her.

488   What do you call a twenty-ton two-headed monster?

Sir.

DOCTOR, DOCTOR

How do you feel when you see hay?

489 **Doctor, Doctor, I have a hoarse throat.**

The resemblance doesn't end there.

490 **Doctor, Doctor, what is the best way to avoid biting insects?**

Don't bite any.

491 **Doctor, Doctor, I feel like a tennis racket.**

You must be too highly strung.

492 **Doctor, Doctor, my nose is running.**

You'd better tie it up then.

493 **Doctor, Doctor, I'm afraid of the dark.**

Then leave the light on.

494 **Doctor, Doctor, I keep stealing things.**

Take one of these pills, and if that doesn't work, bring me back a computer.

495 **Doctor, Doctor, I feel like a pair of socks.**

Well, I'll be darned.

Hey Doc... Can I interest you in my complete boxed set?

496 **Doctor, Doctor, I think I'm a video.**

I thought I'd seen you before.

497 **Doctor, Doctor I keep thinking I'm a yo-yo.**

How are you feeling?

Oh, up and down.

498 **Doctor, Doctor, how can I stop my nose from running?**

Stick your foot out and trip it.

499 **Doctor, Doctor, people keep disagreeing with me.**

No, they don't.

500 **Doctor, Doctor, I'm so ugly. What can I do about it?**

Hire yourself out for Halloween parties.

501 **Doctor, Doctor, I feel run down.**

You should be more careful crossing the road then.

Now who didn't cross at the lights then..?

502 **Doctor, Doctor, I'm at death's door.**

Don't worry, I'll pull you through.

503 **Doctor, Doctor, my stomach is sore.**

Stop your belly aching.

504 **Doctor, Doctor, I'm having trouble breathing.**

I'll put a stop to that.

505 Why do doctors wear masks?

Because if they make a mistake, the person won't
know who did it!

**506 Doctor, Doctor, I feel
like a dog!**

Then go see a vet!

**507 Doctor, Doctor, I
keep thinking I'm
a doorknob.**

Now don't fly off the
handle.

508 **Doctor, Doctor, I'm a wrestler and I feel awful.**

Get a grip on yourself then.

509 **Doctor, Doctor, some days I think I'm a pony.**

Don't worry, you're just a little hoarse.

510 **Doctor, Doctor, I keep thinking I'm a dog.**

How long has this been going on?

Ever since I was a pup.

511 **Doctor, Doctor, everyone hates me.**

Don't be silly, not everyone has met you yet.

512 **Doctor, Doctor, I'm suffering from hallucinations.**

I'm sure you are only imagining it.

513 **Doctor, Doctor, I feel like a piano.**

Wait a moment, while I make some notes.

514 **Doctor, Doctor, will you treat me?**

No, you'll have to pay like everybody else.

515 **Doctor, Doctor, I keep thinking I'm a $10 bill.**

Go shopping, the change will do you good.

516 **Doctor, Doctor, I swallowed a spoon.**

Well, try to relax and don't stir.

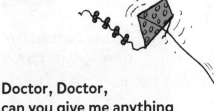

517 **Doctor, Doctor, can you give me anything for excessive wind?**

Sure, here's a kite.

oh...excuse me

518 **Doctor, Doctor, I might be a caterpillar.**

Don't worry, you'll soon change.

Hey Doc... I didn't swallow my kazoo... ...It was in my pocket all along!

519 **Doctor, Doctor, I was playing a kazoo and I swallowed it.**

Lucky you weren't playing the piano.

520 **Doctor, Doctor, nobody ever listens to me.**

Next!

521 **Doctor Doctor, I keep thinking I'm a joke.**

Don't make me laugh.

522 **Doctor Doctor, I'm turning into a trash can.**

Don't talk such rubbish.

523 **Doctor Doctor, I feel like an apple.**

Well, don't worry, I won't bite.

524 **Doctor, Doctor, I feel like a bell.**

Well, take these, and if they don't work, give me a ring.

525 **Doctor, Doctor, I'm as sick as a dog.**

Well, I can't help you because I'm not a vet.

526 Doctor, Doctor, my eyesight is getting worse.

You're absolutely right, this is a post office.

527 Doctor, Doctor, the first thirty minutes I'm up every morning I feel dizzy. What should I do?

Get up half an hour later.

528 Doctor, Doctor, what does this X-ray of my head show?

Unfortunately, nothing.

529 **Doctor, Doctor, this ointment you gave me makes my arm smart!**

Try putting some on your head.

530 **Doctor, Doctor, something is preying on my mind!**

Don't worry, it will probably starve to death.

531 **Doctor, Doctor, I feel like a set of curtains.**

Well, pull yourself together.

532 **Doctor, Doctor, I accidentally ate my pillow.**

Don't be so down in the mouth.

533 **Doctor, Doctor, I have a ringing in my ears!**

Well, answer it.

534 **Doctor, Doctor, every time I stand up I see visions of Mickey Mouse and Pluto, and every time I sit down I see Donald Duck!**

How long have you been having these Disney spells?

535 **Doctor, Doctor, it hurts when I do this!**

Well, don't do that.

536 **Doctor, Doctor, my leg hurts. What can I do?**

Limp.

537 **Doctor, Doctor, I snore so loudly I wake myself up!**

Try sleeping in another room.

538 **When do doctors get angry?**

When they run out of patience (patients).

I think it might be the bait you've eaten

539 **What do you call a surgeon with eight arms?**

A doctopus.

540 **Why did the doctor tiptoe past the medicine cabinet?**

Because she didn't want to wake the sleeping pills!

541 **Doctor, Doctor, everyone thinks I'm a liar.**
I don't believe you.

542 **Doctor, Doctor, I feel like a pack of cards!**
Sit down and I'll deal with you later!

543 **Doctor, Doctor, I have a pain in the eye every time I drink hot chocolate!**
Take the spoon out of your mug before you drink.

544 **Doctor, Doctor, I only have 59 seconds to live!**
Just a minute!

545 **Doctor, Doctor, can you help me out?**
Certainly—which way did you come in?

546 **Doctor, Doctor, I dreamed that I ate a large marshmallow!**
Did you wake up without a pillow?

547 **Doctor, Doctor, I can't sleep at night!**
Just lie on the end of your bed—you'll soon drop off.

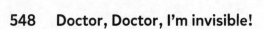

548 Doctor, Doctor, I'm invisible!

I'm sorry, sir, I can't see you right now.

549 Doctor, Doctor, my sister thinks she's a squirrel!

Sounds like a nut case to me.

550 Doctor, Doctor, I think I'm getting shorter!

You'll just have to be a little patient.

551 Doctor, Doctor, did you hear about the boy who swallowed a coin?

No? Well, there's no change yet!

552 **Doctor, Doctor, my son swallowed a pen. What should I do?**

Use a pencil instead!

553 **Doctor, Doctor, I've broken my leg in two places.**

Well, I suggest you don't go back to either of those places!

554 **Doctor, Doctor, my hair is falling out. Can you give me something to keep it in?**

Yes, a paper bag.

555 **Doctor, Doctor, I feel like I'm part of the internet!**

Well, you do look a site.

556 **Doctor, Doctor, I've been turned into a hare.**

Stop rabbiting on about it.

557 **Doctor, Doctor, I keep thinking I'm a dog.**

Well, get up on this couch and I'll examine you.

I can't, I'm not allowed on the furniture.

558 **Doctor, Doctor, can I have a second opinion?**

Of course, come back tomorrow!

559 **Doctor, Doctor, I feel like a window.**

Where's the pane?

560 **Doctor, Doctor, will my measles be better by next Monday?**

I don't want to make any rash promises.

561 **What did one tonsil say to the other tonsil?**

Get dressed up, the doctor is taking us out!

562 **Doctor, Doctor, I keep thinking I'm a fruitcake.**

What's got into you?

Flour, raisins, and cherries.

563 **Doctor, Doctor, you've got to help me, I keep thinking I'm a bridge.**

What's come over you?

So far, a truck, a motorcycle, and two cars.

564 **Doctor, Doctor, I keep hearing a ringing in my ears.**

Where else did you expect to hear it?

565 **Doctor, Doctor, what's good for biting fingernails?**

Very sharp teeth.

FOOD

566 **Waiter, you've got your thumb on my steak!**

Well, I didn't want to drop it again.

567 **Why don't eggs tell jokes?**

They'd crack each other up!

568 **What did the banana sitting in the sun say to the other banana sitting in the sun?**

I don't know about you, but I'm starting to peel.

569 **What do you call a fake noodle?**

An impasta.

570 **What's yellow, brown, and hairy?**

Cheese on toast dropped on the carpet.

571 **What is a cannibal's favorite soup?**

One with a lot of body.

572 **What did the raspberry say to the other raspberry?**

We shouldn't have got into this jam.

573 **Waiter, what is this fly doing in my soup?**

Freestyle, I believe.

574 **How do you fix a broken pizza?**

With tomato paste.

575   **Waiter , there's a fly in my soup!**

Don't worry, sir, the spider in your salad will get it!

576   **What stays hot in the fridge?**

Mustard.

577   **How can you tell the difference between a can of soup and a can of baked beans?**

Read the label.

578   **What has bread on both sides and is afraid of everything?**

A chicken sandwich.

579   **What nut is like a sneeze?**

A cashew.

580 **Hey! There's no chicken in this chicken pot pie.**

Well, do you expect to find dogs in dog biscuits?

581 **Waiter, I'm in a hurry. Will my pizza be long?**

No, it will be round.

582 **Waiter, do you serve crabs in this restaurant?**

Yes, sir, we serve anyone.

583 **Waiter, this soup tastes funny.**

Why aren't you laughing then?

584 **Waiter, this apple pie is squashed.**

Well, you told me to step on it because you were in a hurry.

585 **Waiter, this egg is bad.**

Well, don't blame me, I only laid the table.

586 **Waiter, there is a small insect in my soup!**

Sorry, sir, I'll get you a bigger one!

587 **Why is a pea small and green?**

If it was large and red, it would be a fire engine.

588 **Where do bakers keep their dough?**

In the bank.

589 **Why did the potato cry?**

Because the chips were down.

590 **Waiter, there's a bug in my soup.**

Be quiet, sir, or everyone will want one.

I'd like what he's having please.

591   Why did the baby cookie cry?

Because his mother was a wafer so long.

592   Waiter, do you have frogs legs?

No, I've always walked like this.

The secret to making great wine...

dirty feet

593   What do you get when you step on a grape?

A little wine.

594   What did the teddy bear say when he was offered dessert?

No thanks, I'm stuffed!

NO!... not even a little mint

595 **Have you heard the joke about the butter?**

I'd better not tell you—you might spread it.

596 **Two sausages are in a pan. One looks at the other and says, "Gosh, it's hot in here," and the other sausage says,**

"Goodness gracious, it's a talking sausage!"

Ahhr stop griping and just sizzle away quietly like the rest of us!

597 **Mom, can I have a dollar for the man who's crying in the park?**

What's he crying about?

He's crying, "Hot dogs, one dollar."

598 **What's the difference between pea soup and roast chicken?**

Anyone can roast chicken.

599 **Johnny, I think your dog likes me. He's been looking at me all night.**

That's because you're eating out of his bowl.

600 **What's long, green, and slowly turns red?**

A cucumber holding its breath.

601 What do you make from baked beans and onions?

Tear gas.

602 Waiter, how long will my sausages be?

Oh, about 3 inches.

603 How do you fix a cracked pumpkin?

With a pumpkin patch!

604 **Waiter, there's a fly in my soup.**

Yes, sir, the hot water killed it.

605 **Why did the jello wobble?**

Because it saw the apple turnover.

606 **What is red and goes up and down?**

A tomato in an elevator!

607 **Why did the man at the orange juice factory lose his job?**

He couldn't concentrate!

608 **How do you make an elephant sandwich?**

Well, first, you take an enormous loaf of bread ...

609 **Why are cooks mean?**

Because they beat the eggs and whip the cream!

610 **Why is a psychiatrist like a squirrel?**

Because he's surrounded by nuts.

611 **Why should you never tell secrets in a grocery store?**

Because the corn has ears, potatoes have eyes, and beanstalk.

612 **Waiter, bring me something to eat and make it snappy.**

How about an alligator sandwich, sir?

613 **Why did the cleaning woman quit?**

Because grime doesn't pay.

614 **Why did the raisin go out with the prune?**

Because he couldn't find a date.

615 **Why did Robin Hood rob the rich?**

The poor didn't have any money.

616   What do you get if you cross a burglar with a cement mixer?

A hardened criminal.

617   If I had six grapefruit in one hand and seven in the other, what would I have?

Very big hands.

618   How do you make a sausage roll?

Push it down a hill.

619   What did the cannibal have for breakfast?

Baked beings.

There goes your Father again!

620   What did the baby corn say to the mother corn?

"Where's pop corn?"

621   What did one plate say to the other plate?

"Lunch is on me!"

622   Why did the baker stop making doughnuts?

Because he was sick of the whole business.

GROSS

623 **How do you make a hankie dance?**

Put some boogie into it.

624 **What is the soft stuff between a shark's teeth?**

Slow swimmers.

625 **Mommy, Mommy, can I lick the bowl?**

No! You'll have to flush like everyone else.

626 **Why are sausages so bad mannered?**

They spit in the frying pan.

627 **Why are basketball players never asked for dinner?**

Because they're always dribbling!

628 **What's the difference between a maggot and a cockroach?**

Cockroaches crunch more when you eat them.

629 **What's green, sticky, and smells like eucalyptus?**

Koala vomit.

630 **What do you get if you cross an elephant with a box of laxatives?**

Out of the way.

Do you smell eucalyptus?

631 **What is the difference between broccoli and boogers?**

Kids don't like to eat broccoli!

632 **Why did Piglet look in the toilet?**

He was looking for Pooh.

633 **What do you find up a clean nose?**

Fingerprints.

634 **What's invisible and smells of carrots?**

Bunny farts!

635 **What's the last thing that goes through a bug's mind when he hits a car windscreen?**

His rear end.

636 **Why do little brothers chew with their mouths open?**

Flies have got to live somewhere.

637 **How do you keep flies out of the kitchen?**

Put a pile of manure in the living room!

638 **What's the difference between a worm and an apple?**

Have you ever tried worm pie?

639 **How can you tell when a moth farts?**
He flies straight for a second.

Yeee-hah!

640 **What has two gray legs and two brown legs?**
An elephant with diarrhea.

641 **What makes you seasick?**
Your little brother's vomit.

642 **What is worse than finding a maggot in your apple?**
Finding half a maggot!

643 **What's another name for a snail?**
A booger with a crash helmet.

644 **What's yellow and smells of bananas?**
Monkey vomit.

WORLD LAND SPEED RECORD
ATTEMPT

645 **What's green and red and goes at 70 mph?**
A frog in a blender.

646 **What has fifty legs and can't walk?**
Half a centipede.

JUST SILLY

647 **How do you know when a doofus has been making chocolate chip cookies?**

There are M&M shells on the floor!

648 **How did the doofus fall on the floor?**

He tripped over the cordless vacuum cleaner.

649 **Why did the doofus break into two windows?**

One to go in and the other to go out.

650 **What's that on your shoulder?**
A birthmark.
How long have you had it?

651 **What happened to the doofus who couldn't tell the difference between oatmeal and putty?**
All his windows fell out.

652 **What did the farmer say when he lost his tractor?**
"Where's my tractor?"

653 **Why did the doofus climb the glass wall?**
To see what was on the other side!

654 **Why did the doofus get fired from the banana factory?**

He threw out all the bent ones.

655 **Why was the doofus hitting his head against the wall?**

Because it felt so good when he stopped!

656 **How many fools does it take to screw in a light bulb?**

Three ... one to hold the bulb, and two to turn the chair!

657 How do you confuse a doofus?

Put him in a round room and tell him to sit in the corner!

658 How do you get a one-armed doofus out of a tree?

Wave to him.

Hi

659 What do you do if a doofus throws a hand grenade at you?

Pull the pin and throw it back.

660 What do you mean by telling everyone that I'm an idiot?

I'm sorry, I didn't know it was supposed to be a secret!

Ahhrr... doofus doesn't have two O's

661 How can you tell when a doofus has been using the computer?

There is whiteout all over the screen!

662 What did the stupid burglar do when he saw a "WANTED" poster outside the police station?

He went in and applied for the job!

663 **How do you keep a doofus in suspense?**

I'll tell you tomorrow!

664 **How did the doofus break his arm while raking leaves?**

He fell out of the tree!

665 **Why did the doofus get fired from the M&M factory?**

Because he threw away all the W's!

666 **Why did the doofus sleep under his car?**

So he would wake up oily in the morning.

667 How do you sink a submarine full of fools?

Knock on the door.

668 Why was the fool's brain the size of a pea after exercising?

It swelled up!

669 What happened to the foolish tap dancer?

She fell in the sink.

670 Did you hear the one about the silly fox that got stuck in a trap?

She chewed off three legs and was still stuck.

671 **Why was the doofus covered in bruises?**

He started to walk through a revolving door and then changed his mind!

672 **What is the difference between a doofus and a shopping cart?**

Shopping carts have a mind of their own.

673 **Why did the doofus go in the ditch?**

Her turn signal was on.

674 **Three tourists were driving down the highway trying to get to Disneyland. They saw a sign that read:**

"Disneyland Left." So they went home.

675 **How do you know if a doofus sent you an email?**

There's a stamp on it.

676 **Did you hear about the doofus who did bird impressions?**

He ate worms.

677 **Why did the doofus leap out of the window?**

To try his new jump suit.

678 **Why did the fool cross the road?**

To get to the middle.

679 **Why did the fool put a chicken in a hot bath?**

So she would lay hard-boiled eggs.

680 **How do you make a doofus laugh on a Sunday?**

Tell him a joke on Saturday.

681 **How can you tell when there's a doofus on an oil rig?**

He's the one throwing bread to the helicopters.

682 Why did the doofus buy a chess set?
He was saving it for a brainy day.

683 What did the foolish ghost do?
Climbed over walls.

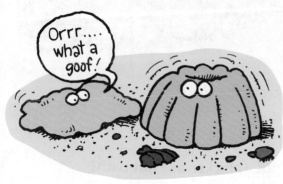

684 What happened to the stupid jellyfish?
It set.

685 Stop! This is a one-way street!
Well, I'm only going one way!

686 Did you hear about the doofus who paid five dollars to have his thoughts read?
He got his money back.

687 What did the doofus call his pet zebra?
Spot.

688 **Did you hear about the doofus who got a boomerang for his birthday?**

He spent the next two days trying to throw the old one away.

689 **Did you hear about the bungee jumper who shot up and down for 3 hours before they could bring him under control?**

He had a yo-yo in his pocket!

690 **What's red and hangs in an orange tree?**

A silly strawberry.

SILLY

INVENTIONS

691 An ejector seat on a helicopter.

692 A parachute that opens on impact.

693 Waterproof teabags.

You know... I've used this tea bag over 250 times... I think the secret's in the plastic coating

694 A left-handed screwdriver.

695 A one-way escalator.

KNOCK-KNOCK

696 **Knock-Knock.**
Who's there?
Cargo.
Cargo who?
Car go beep beep!

697 **Knock-Knock.**
Who's there?
Alison.
Alison who?
Alison to the radio.

698 **Knock-Knock.**
Who's there?
Police.
Police who?
Police let me in.

699 **Knock-Knock.**
Who's there?
Gotter.
Gotter who?
Gotter go to the toilet.

700 **Knock-Knock.**
Who's there?
Mister.
Mister who?
Mister last train home.

701 **Knock-Knock.**
Who's there?
My panther.
My panther who?
My panther falling down.

702 **Knock-Knock.**
Who's there?
Aardvark.
Aardvark who?
Aardvark a million miles for one of your smiles!

703 **Knock-Knock.**
Who's there?
Caterpillar.
Caterpillar who?
Cat-er-pillar of feline society.

704 **Knock-Knock.**
Who's there?
Norma Lee.
Norma Lee who?
Norma Lee I'd be at school, but I've got the day off.

705 **Knock-Knock.**
Who's there?
Gladys.
Gladys who?
Gladys Saturday, aren't you?

706 **Knock-Knock.**
Who's there?
Witches.
Witches who?
Witches the way home?

Come on baby start...!

707 **Knock-Knock.**
Who's there?
Lettuce.
Lettuce who?
Lett-uce in, it's cold outside.

708 **Knock-Knock.**
Who's there?
Tank.
Tank who?
You're welcome.

709 **Knock-Knock.**
Who's there?
Turnip.
Turnip who?
Turnip for school tomorrow or there will be trouble.

710 **Knock-Knock.**
Who's there?
Sawyer.
Sawyer who?
Sawyer lights on, thought I'd drop by.

711 **Knock-Knock.**
Who's there?
Freeze.
Freeze who?
Freeze a jolly good fellow.

712   **Knock-Knock.**
Who's there?
Turnip.
Turnip who?
Turnip the heater, it's cold in here!

713   **Knock-Knock.**
Who's there?
Scott.
Scott who?
Scott nothing to do with you.

714   **Knock-Knock.**
Who's there?
Robin.
Robin who?
Robin you! So hand over your cash.

715 **Knock-Knock.**
Who's there?
Roach.
Roach who?
Roach you a letter, but I didn't send it.

716 **Knock-Knock.**
Who's there?
Hanover.
Hanover who?
Hanover all your money!

717 **Knock-Knock.**
Who's there?
Nanna.
Nanna who?
Nanna your business.

718 **Knock-Knock.**
Who's there?
Luke.
Luke who?
Luke through the peephole and you'll see.

719 **Knock-Knock.**
Who's there?
Boo.
Boo who?
What are you crying about?

720 **Knock-Knock.**
Who's there?
Eiffel.
Eiffel who?
Eiffel down.

721 **Knock-Knock.**
Who's there?
Justin.
Justin who?
Justin time for lunch.

I'm on a diet for my weight....

722 **Knock-Knock.**
Who's there?
Nobel.
Nobel who?
No bell so I just knocked.

723 **Knock-Knock.**
Who's there?
Minnie.
Minnie who?
Minnie people would like to know.

724 **Knock-Knock.**
Who's there?
Troy.
Troy who?
Troy as I may, I can't reach the bell.

725 **Knock-Knock.**
Who's there?
Kenya.
Kenya who?
Kenya keep the noise down, some of us are trying to sleep.

726 **Knock-Knock.**
Who's there?
Iran.
Iran who?
Iran 25 laps around the track, and boy, am I tired!

727 **Knock-Knock.**
Who's there?
Avon.
Avon who?
Avon you to open the door.

728 **Knock-Knock.**
Who's there?
Lionel.
Lionel who?
Lionel bite you if you don't watch out.

729 **Knock-Knock.**
Who's there?
Cows.
Cows who?
No, cows moo!

730 **Knock-Knock.**
Who's there?
Border patrol.
Border patrol who?
We ask the questions here!

731 **Knock-Knock.**
Who's there?
Ice cream!
Ice cream who?
Ice cream, you scream!

732 **Knock-Knock.**
Who's there?
Pencil.
Pencil who?
If you don't wear a belt, your PENCIL fall down!

733 **Knock-Knock.**
Who's there?
Tish.
Tish who?
Bless you!

734 **Knock-Knock.**
Who's there?
Shelby!
Shelby who?
Shelby comin' round the mountain when she comes!

735 **Knock-Knock.**
Who's there?
Dewayne!
Dewayne who?
Dewayne the bathtub before I dwown!

736 **Knock-Knock.**
Who's there?
Midas.
Midas who?
Midas well let me in.

737   **Knock-Knock.**

Who's there?

Euripedes.

Euripedes who?

Euripedes pants, Eumenides pants.

738   **Knock-Knock.**

Who's there?

Miniature.

Miniature who?

Miniature let me in, I'll tell you.

739   **Knock-Knock.**

Who's there?

Arch!

Arch who?

Bless you!

740   **Knock-Knock.**

Who's there?

Max.

Max who?

Max no difference who it is—just open the door!

741   **Knock-Knock.**

Who's there?

Howard.

Howard who?

Howard I know?

742   **Knock-Knock.**
Who's there?
Red!
Red who?
Knock-Knock.
Who's there?
Red!
Red who?
Knock-Knock.
Who's there?
Red!
Red who?
Knock-Knock.
Who's there?
Red!
Red who?
Knock-Knock.
Who's there?
Orange!
Orange who?
**Orange you glad
I didn't say red?**

743   **Knock-Knock.**
Who's there?
Little old lady.
Little old lady who?
**I didn't know you
could yodel!**

744   **Knock-Knock.**
Who's there?
Artichokes.
Artichokes who?
Artichokes when he eats too fast!

745   **Knock-Knock.**
Who's there?
Letter.
Letter who?
Letter in or she'll knock the door down.

...and whatever you do.... don't call her 'dear'...

746   **Knock-Knock.**
Who's there?
Tuba.
Tuba who?
Tuba toothpaste.

747   **Knock-Knock.**
Who's there?
Phyllis.
Phyllis who?
Phyllis a glass of water, will you?

748 **Knock-Knock.**
Who's there?
Still.
Still who?
Still knocking.

749 **Knock-Knock.**
Who's there?
Avenue.
Avenue who?
Avenue heard these jokes before?

I'll come back again tomorrow... and the day after too!

750 **Knock-Knock.**
Who's there?
Wayne.
Wayne who?
Wayne, Wayne, go away, come again another day!

751 **Knock-Knock.**
Who's there?
Debate!
Debate who?
Debate goes on de hook if you want to catch de fish!

752 **Knock-Knock.**
Who's there?
Ben.
Ben who?
Ben knocking on the door all afternoon!

753 **Knock-Knock.**
Who's there?
Ammonia.
Ammonia who?
Ammonia little girl who can't reach the door bell!

I thought you were a little bug..

754 **Knock-Knock.**
Who's there?
Will.
Will who?
Will you be my valentine?

755 **Knock-Knock.**
Who's there?
Water.
Water who?
Water friends for!

756 **Knock-Knock.**
Who's there?
William.
William who?
William mind your own business?

757 Knock-Knock.
Who's there?
Smore.
Smore who?
Can I have smore marshmallows?

758 Knock-Knock.
Who's there?
Arncha.
Arncha who?
Arncha going to let me in? It's freezing out here!

759 Knock-Knock.
Who's there?
M-2.
M-2 who?
M-2 tired to knock!

760 Knock-Knock.
Who's there?
The Sultan.
The Sultan who?
The Sultan Pepper.

761 **Knock-Knock.**
Who's there?
Waiter.
Waiter who?
Waiter minute while I tie my shoe.

762 **Knock-Knock.**
Who's there?
Army.
Army who?
Army and you still friends?

763 **Knock-Knock.**
Who's there?
Wooden shoe.
Wooden shoe who?
Wooden shoe like to know.

764 **Knock-Knock.**
Who's there?
Wednesday.
Wednesday who?
Wednesday saints go marching in!

765 **Knock-Knock.**
Who's there?
Jamaica.
Jamaica who?
Jamaica mistake?

766 **Knock-Knock.**
Who's there?
Who.
Who who?
What are you—an owl?

767 **Knock-Knock.**
Who's there?
Ice cream soda.
Ice cream soda who?
Ice cream soda neighbors wake up!

768 **Knock-Knock.**
Who's there?
Shamp.
Shamp who?
Why, is my hair dirty?

769 **Knock-Knock.**
Who's there?
Empty.
Empty who?
Empty V (MTV).

770 **Knock-Knock.**
Who's there?
Vitamin.
Vitamin who?
Vitam in for a party!

771 **Knock-Knock.**
Who's there?
Despair.
Despair who?
Despair tire is flat.

772 **Knock-Knock.**
Who's there?
Icon.
Icon who?
Icon tell you another knock-knock joke. Do you want me to?

773 **Knock-Knock.**
Who's there?
House.
House who?
House it going?

774 **Knock-Knock.**
Who's there?
Closure.
Closure who?
Closure mouth when you're eating!

775 **Knock-Knock.**
Who's there?
Icy.
Icy who?
Icy your underwear.

776   **Knock-Knock.**
Who's there?
Tick.
Tick who?
Tick 'em up, I'm a tongue-tied towboy.

777   **Knock-Knock.**
Who's there?
Dishes.
Dishes who?
Dishes a very bad joke!

778   **Knock-Knock.**
Who's there?
Weed.
Weed who?
Weed better mow the lawn before it gets too long.

779 **Knock-Knock.**

Who's there?

Alaska.

Alaska who?

Alaska one more time ... let me in!

780 **Knock-Knock.**

Who's there?

Catch.

Catch who?

God bless you!

Would it be possible to have my SAMPLE LIPSTICK and my foot back, please?

Door to Door COSMETICS

781 **Knock-Knock.**

Who's there?

Madam.

Madam who?

Madam foot got stuck in the door.

782 **Knock-Knock.**

Who's there?

Howdy!

Howdy who?

Howdy do that?

783 **Knock-Knock.**

Who's there?

Leaf.

Leaf who?

Leaf me alone.

784 **Knock-Knock.**
Who's there?
Butcher.
Butcher who?
Butcher arms around me!

785 **Knock-Knock.**
Who's there?
Stopwatch.
Stopwatch who?
Stopwatch you're doing and open this door!

786 **Knock-Knock.**
Who's there?
Winner.
Winner who?
Winner you gonna get this door fixed?

787 **Knock-Knock.**
Who's there?
Weirdo.
Weirdo who?
Weirdo you think you're going?

788 **Knock-Knock.**
Who's there?
Canoe.
Canoe who?
Canoe come out to play?

789 **Knock-Knock.**
Who's there?
Radio.
Radio who?
Radio not, here I come!

790 **Knock-Knock.**
Who's there?
Accordion.
Accordion who?
Accordion to the TV, it's going to rain tomorrow.

791 **Knock-Knock.**
Who's there?
Irish.
Irish who?
Irish I had a million dollars.

792 **Knock-Knock.**
Who's there?
Alex.
Alex who?
Alexplain later, just let me in.

793 **Knock-Knock.**
Who's there?
Zombies.
Zombies who?
Zombies make honey, zombies just buzz around.

794 **Knock-Knock.**
Who's there?
Cameron.
Cameron who?
Cameron a smile are all you need to take pictures.

795 **Knock-Knock.**
Who's there?
Abbot.
Abbot who?
Abbot you don't know who this is!

796 **Knock-Knock.**
Who's there?
Adore.
Adore who?
Adore is between us, open up!

797 **Knock-Knock.**
Who's there?
Sombrero.
Sombrero who?
**"Sombrero-ver
the rainbow ..."**

eet eez such
a love-el-ly day.....
eet makes me want to sing!

798 **Knock-Knock.**
Who's there?
Alaska.
Alaska who?
Alaska no questions. You tella no lies.

799 **Knock-Knock.**
Who's there?
Irish stew.
Irish stew who?
Irish stew in the name of the law.

800 **Knock-Knock.**
Who's there?
Orson.
Orson who?
Orson cart!

801 **Knock-Knock.**
Who's there?
Felix.
Felix who?
Felix my ice cream, I'll lick his.

802 **Knock-Knock.**
Who's there?
Cornflakes.
Cornflakes who?
I'll tell you tomorrow, it's a cereal.

803 **Knock-Knock.**
Who's there?
Haywood, Hugh, and Harry.
Haywood, Hugh, and Harry who?
Haywood Hugh Harry up and open the door!

804 **Knock-Knock.**
Who's there?
Arthur.
Arthur who?
Arthur anymore jelly beans in the jar?

805 **Knock-Knock.**
Who's there?
Theresa.
Theresa who?
Theresa green.

806 **Knock-Knock.**
Who's there?
Wilma.
Wilma who?
Wilma dinner be ready soon?

Change the channel on the TV, will you luv... my battery's dead again

807   **Knock-Knock.**
Who's there?
Abbott!
Abbott who?
Abbott time you opened this door!

O.K..O.K..O.K...
An 'ABBOTT'
might be
stretching
the truth
a little

808   **Knock-Knock.**
Who's there?
Oscar.
Oscar who?
Oscar silly question, get a silly answer.

809   **Knock-Knock.**
Who's there?
Sancho.
Sancho who?
Sancho a letter, but you never answered.

Good night, Frank...

Good night, Celia.... The alligator of my dreams.

810   **Knock-Knock.**
Who's there?
Celia.
Celia who?
Celia later alligator.

811   **Knock-Knock.**
Who's there?
Betty.
Betty who?
Betty late than never.

812 **Knock-Knock.**
Who's there?
Snow.
Snow who?
Snow good asking me.

813 **Knock-Knock.**
Who's there?
Satin.
Satin who?
Who satin my chair?

814 **Knock-Knock.**
Who's there?
Barbie.
Barbie who?
Barbie Q.

815 **Knock-Knock.**

Who's there?

Carrie.

Carrie who?

Carrie me inside, I'm exhausted.

816 **Knock-Knock.**

Who's there?

Irish.

Irish who?

Irish I knew some more knock-knock jokes.

RIDDLES

817 **What are two things you cannot have for breakfast?**

Lunch and dinner.

818 **Why did the boy throw butter out the window?**

Because he wanted to see a butterfly!

819 **What has eyes that cannot see, a tongue that cannot taste, and a soul that cannot die?**

A shoe.

820 **What can you hear but not see, and only speaks when it is spoken to?**

An echo.

821 **What did the fisherman say to the magician?**

Pick a cod, any cod.

822   **What ten letter word starts with gas?**
A-U-T-O-M-O-B-I-L-E.

823   **How many apples can you put in an empty box?**
One. After that, it's not empty anymore.

824   **When will water stop flowing downhill?**
When it reaches the bottom.

825   **What is there more of the less you see?**
Darkness.

826   **What's easier to give than receive?**
Criticism.

827   **If April showers bring May flowers, what do May flowers bring?**
Pilgrims!

828 **Where can you always find a helping hand?**
At the end of your arm.

829 **Why do firefighters wear red suspenders?**
To keep their pants up.

Can you give me a hand?

830 **What kind of dress can never be worn?**
Your address.

831 **What weighs more—a pound of lead or a pound of feathers?**
They both weigh the same.

832 **What word is always spelled incorrectly?**
Incorrectly.

833 **What has a bottom at the top?**
A leg.

834 **Why is milk the fastest thing in the world?**

Because it's pasteurized before you see it.

835 **What sort of ring is always square?**

A boxing ring!

836 **What's the last thing you take off before bed?**

Your feet off the floor.

837 **What starts with an E, ends with an E, and only has one letter in it?**

An envelope!

838 **What is always coming but never arrives?**
Tomorrow.

839 **What did the piece of wood say to the drill?**
You bore me.

840 **What can you serve but never eat?**
A volleyball.

841 **What do you put in a barrel to make it lighter?**
A hole.

842 **What stays in the corner and travels all around the world?**
A postage stamp.

843 **What do you call a bee that is always complaining?**
A grumble bee!

844 **What's taken before you get it?**
Your picture.

845 Which room has no door, no windows, no floor, and no roof?

A mushroom!

846 What gets wet the more you dry?

A towel!

847 What's green, has eight legs, and would kill you if it fell on you from out of a tree?

A pool table.

848 What washes up on very small beaches?

Microwaves!

849 What breaks when you say it?

Silence!

850 What gets bigger and bigger as you take more away from it?

A hole!

851   What bow can't be tied?
A rainbow!

852   Why are false teeth like stars?
They come out at night.

853   Why do you go to bed?
Because the bed will not come to you.

854   What goes all around a pasture but never moves?
A fence!

855   What is H2O4?
Drinking!

856   What has teeth but cannot eat?
A comb!

857   What can you hold without touching?
Your breath.

858 **What question can you never answer yes to?**

Are you asleep?

859 **What is the only true cure for dandruff?**

Baldness!

860 **What is big, red, and eats rocks?**

A big red rock eater!

861 **What goes all around the world but doesn't move?**

The Equator.

862 **What starts with a P, ends with an E, and has a million letters in it?**

Post Office!

863 **What is always behind the times?**

The back of a watch.

864 **Why can't it rain for two days in a row?**

Because there is a night in between.

865 **What goes up and does not come down?**

Your age!

866 **What was the highest mountain before Mt. Everest was discovered?**

Mt. Everest.

867 **What goes up and down but never moves?**

A flight of stairs.

868 **How many seconds are there in a year?**

12 ... 2nd of January, 2nd of February ...!

869 Which candle burns longer—a red one or a green one?

Neither, they both burn shorter!

870 What runs across the floor without legs?

Water.

871 Which is the longest rope?

Europe!

GO EASY!!

872 What has holes and holds water?

A sponge.

873 What puzzles make you angry?

Crossword puzzles.

874 **What runs but doesn't get anywhere?**
A refrigerator.

875 **What do you call a superb painting done by a rat?**
A mouseterpiece!

876 **What kind of ship never sinks?**
Friendship!

877 **What has four fingers and a thumb but is not a hand?**
A glove!

878 **What cup can you never drink out of?**
A hiccup.

879 **What kind of coat can you put on only when it's wet?**
A coat of paint.

880 **What belongs to you but is used more by other people?**
Your name.

881 **What kind of cup can't hold water?**
A cupcake.

882 **What weapon was most feared by medieval knights?**

A can opener.

883 **When things go wrong, what can you always count on?**

Your fingers.

884 **What flies around all day but never goes anywhere?**

A flag.

885 **Where were potatoes first found?**

In the ground.

886 **What can you give away but also keep?**
A cold.

887 **What bet can never be won?**
The alphabet.

888 **What has two hands, no fingers, stands still, and runs?**
A clock.

889 **What is the beginning of eternity, the end of time, the beginning of every ending?**
The letter "E."

890 **How long should a person's legs be?**
Long enough to reach their feet.

891 **What can't walk but can run?**
A river.

892 **When is it bad luck to be followed by a big black cat?**
When you are a little gray mouse.

SPORT

893 **Why did the golfer wear two pairs of pants?**

In case he got a hole in one.

894 **What does every winner lose in a race?**

Their breath.

895 **Why is a scrambled egg bad at sport?**

It always gets beaten.

896 **What are the four seasons?**

Baseball, basketball, soccer, and football!

897 **What has 22 legs and two wings but can't fly?**

A soccer team.

898 **Where do old bowling balls end up?**

In the gutter!

899 **What illness do martial artists get?**

Kung Flu.

900 **What position did the pile of wood play on the football team?**

De-fence!

901 **When is a baby like a basketball player?**

When he dribbles.

902 **Why was the boxer known as Picasso?**

Because he spent all his time on the canvas.

903 **Why did the runner wear rippled sole shoes?**

To give the ants a fifty-fifty chance.

904 **What did one bowling ball say to the other?**

Don't stop me, I'm on a roll.

905 **What's a ghost's favorite position in soccer?**

Ghoul-keeper.

906 **What happens when baseball players get old?**

They go batty.

907 **Why were the arrows nervous?**

Because they were all in a quiver.

908 **What do you get when you cross a football player with a gorilla?**

I don't know, but nobody tries to stop it from scoring.

909   **Why did all the bowling pins go down?**

Because they were on strike.

910   **Why do soccer players have so much trouble eating?**

They think they can't use their hands.

911   **Why was the centipede two hours late for the soccer match?**

It took him two hours to put his shoes on.

912   **Why are basketball players always so cool?**

Because of all the fans.

913   **Why was the chickens' soccer match a bad idea?**

Because there were too many fowls.

GO GO GO..THE FREE-RANGE HENS.'

914   **Why is tennis such a noisy game?**

Because everyone raises a racket.

915   **Why is Cinderella so bad at sport?**

Because she has a pumpkin for a coach and she runs away from the ball.

COMPUTERS

916 **Why was the computer so tired when it got home?**

Because it had a hard drive!

917 **Why was there beef stew on the laptop?**

It was in a wireless hotpot.

918 **What did the computer say when a man typed something in on the keyboard?**

You're really pushing my buttons, little man!

919 **How many programmers does it take to screw in a light bulb?**

None, it's a hardware problem!

920 **Where do you find the biggest spider?**

In the world wide web.

921 Why did the computer cross the road?

Because it was programmed by the chicken.

922 What do you get if you cross a computer programmer with an athlete?

A diskus thrower.

923 Hey, did you see who stole my computer?

Yes, he went data way!

924 Why did the computer sneeze?

It had a virus.

925 What did the computer say to the programmer at lunchtime?

Can I have a byte?

926 What do computers do when they get hungry?

They eat computer chips.

927 Why was the computer cold?

Because it left its Windows open.

WHAT DO YOU CALL...

928   ... a man who likes to work out?

Jim!

929   ... a girl with a tennis racket on her head?

Annette!

930   ... a woman with a cat on her head?

Kitty!

931   ... a man with a seagull on his head?

Cliff!

932   ... a boy hanging on the wall?

Art!

933 ... a man with a map on his head?

Miles!

934 ... a man with a car on his head?

Jack!

935 ... a man who owes money?

Bill!

936 ... a man with a spade?

Doug!

937 ... a man without a spade?

Douglas!

938 ... a girl with a frog on her head?

Lily!

939 ... a man in a pile of leaves?

Russell!

940 ... a woman in the distance?

Dot!

941 ... a man with a Christmas tree on his head?

Noel.

942 ... a woman with a Christmas tree on her head?

Carol.

943 ... a boy holding a calculator?

Adam!

944 ... a man with rabbits in his trousers?

Warren.

SILLY BOOK TITLES

945   "The Invisible Man" by Peter Out.

946   "How to be Taller" by Stan Dupp.

947   "A Terrible Nightmare" by Gladys Over.

948   "Famous Frights" by Terry Fied.

949   "Strong Winds" by Gail Forse.

950   "Swimming the English Channel" by Frances Neer.

951   "World Atlas" by Joe Graffie.

952   "Speaking French" by Lorna Lang Wedge.

953   "Close Shaves" by Ray Zerr.

954   "Great Eggspectations" by Charles Chickens.

955   "How to be Shorter" by Neil Down.

956   "Rice Growing" by Paddy Field.

957   "Horror Stories" by R. U. Scared.

958   "Up the Amazon" by P. Rhana.

959   "The Unknown Author" by Anne Onymous.

960   "The Long Walk to School" by Mr. Bus.

961   "Infectious Diseases" by Willie Catchit.

962   "Exercise At Home" by Ben Dan Stretch.

963   "A Bullfighter's Life" by Matt Adore.

964   "Broken Window" by Eva Brick.

965 "The Mad Cat" by Claud Boddy.

966 "Egyptian Mummies" by M. Barmer.

967 "Hungry Dog" by Nora Bone.

968 "A Hole in the Bucket" by Lee King.

969 "Camping in Iceland" by I. C. Blast.

970 "The Poltergeist" by Eve L. Spirit.

971 "A Ghost in the Attic" by Howie Wales.

972   "Explosives for Beginners"
by Dinah Might.

973   "Ghosts and Ghouls" by Sue Pernatural.

974   "The Omen" by B. Warned.

975   "Famous Mistakes" by Hugh Did-Watt.

976   "Clairvoyance Made Easy" by I. C. Spooks.

977   "Sahara Journey" by Rhoda Camel.

978   "Jail Break" by Freida Prizner.

979   "The Arctic Ocean" by I. C. Waters.

980 "The Haunted House" by Hugo First.

981 "Stormy Day" by A. Pauline Weather.

982 "Dealing With Bullies" by Howard U. Lykett.

983 "The Billionaire" by Iva Fortune.

984 "Easy Money" by Robin Banks.

985 "Roof Repairs" by Lee King.

986   "A Sting in the Tale" by B. Keeper.

987   "The Rainforest" by Teresa Green.

988   "Across the Savannah" by Ann T. Lope.

989   "Quick Snacks" by Roland Butter.

990   "Crossing Roads Safely" by Luke Bothways.

VEHICLES

991 **What happened to the wooden car with wooden wheels and a wooden engine?**

It wooden go.

This one's a real beauty...made from sustainable forests too!
It's got everything! Solid timber construction
full wood interior...4 good wheels
and....by the look of it....
TERMITES

992 **What did the traffic light say to the car?**

Don't look now, I'm changing.

993 **What flies and wobbles?**

A jellocopter.

994   Why can't a bicycle stand up?
Because it's two tired.

995   When is a car not a car?
When it turns into a garage.

996   What's a fjord?
A Norwegian car.

997 What do you give a sick car?
A fuel injection.

998 How can you find a lost train?
Follow its tracks.

999 What kind of car did Elvis drive?
A Rock-n-Rolls Royce.

1000 **Policeman: Did you know that you were driving at 120 mph?**

Driver: Impossible. I've only been in the car for five minutes.

1001 **What do you call an expensive car with a cheap name?**

A poor-sche.